We thank the following friends for their generous support:

THE MILES GROUP, INC.

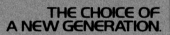

THE CHOICE OF
A NEW GENERATION.

 Apple Computer, Inc. and **ComputerLand® of ElPaso**,
an 🍎 Authorized Education Sales Consultant

GRAMBLING ⊗ MOUNCE
A PROFESSIONAL CORPORATION
ATTORNEYS AND COUNSELORS AT LAW

KPMG Peat Marwick

Providence Memorial Hospital
El Paso's Center for Healthcare Excellence.

A Rainbow in a Tree Publication

Photography by
MICHAEL R. MOSES

Text by
ALEX APOSTOLIDES

Design by
RAYMOND GARTON

Illustrations by
DANIELLE M. MOSES

The FRANKLIN MOUNTAINS

Beginning of the Rockies

Special thanks to —

Victor Mireles, Georgianne Bouillon, Jim Klaes, Malcolm Harris, El Paso Community Foundation, El Paso Zoological Society, El Paso Sierra Club, Americana Museum and El Paso Audubon Society.

Library of Congress Cataloging-in-Publication Data

Main entry under title.
  THE FRANKLIN MOUNTAINS: Beginning of the Rockies
First Printing: September 1990.
ISBN Number: 0-944551-01-7

1. United States — Description and travel 1990 — Views.
2. United States — Photography, Nature.
3. United States — Southwest, Environment, Ecology.

10 9 8 7 6 5 4 3 2 1

THE FRANKLIN MOUNTAINS: Beginning of the Rockies was created using an Apple® Macintosh® computer, Apple LaserWriter IINT®, Linotronic L300® imagesetter, Aldus PageMaker® and Microsoft Word®. The typefaces used in this book are Adobe® Systems' Galliard, Caslon 540, Caslon 3, and Caslon OpenFace.

Printed in El Paso, Texas
by Wilmot Printing Company, Inc.,
A Better Printing Company
United States of America

Franklin Mountains: Beginning of the Rockies, with Sierra de Juárez in the background (pages 2-3).

Five feet off the pavement, you're in the middle of the wilderness (pages 4-5).

This is the Pass of the North—city, mountains and river intertwined (pages 6-7).

The Franklins loom over the greens of the Coronado Country Club (pages 16-17).

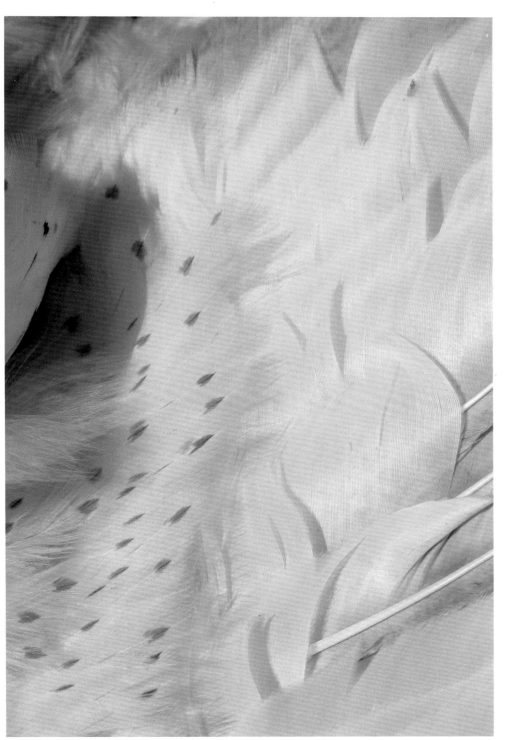

Dedicated to

LIVING ON THE DESERT

*the earth science
of preserving
a fragile ecology;*

*the social act
of seeing arid beauty;*

and

*the personal responsibility
of intimate intercourse
with nature.*

Contents

FACE TO FACE

*O*ur High Desert Valley is a unique blend of intriguing mixtures—a wonderful composite—many cultures—two states—two countries. An unusual metropolitan area with an image that goes back over 400 years...once only a path, a connection...a pass to the north...El Paso, Las Cruces and Juárez, sisters mesmerized by the sun, tranquilized by a unique climate, looking for self identity...still, and always, The Pass...vital, proud, distinct and isolated.

KVIA television is working for this wonderful country, growing together with our cosmopolitan culture at the beginning of the Rockies... 7-together cares.

*g*rambling & Mounce, A Professional Corporation, traces its roots in El Paso to the turn of the century. We have always been dedicated to providing superior legal services to our clientele; and, in the course of providing these services, we have developed strong ties to the community and a lasting concern for our surroundings.

The Franklin Mountains contribute to the unique character of El Paso and will continue to be a spectacular treasure for generations to come. We have implemented a firm-wide recycling program as a part of our ongoing commitment to El Paso, and we hope that the recent emphasis on environmental awareness and education encourages others to do the same. We are pleased to participate in the publication of this book and hope you join with us in celebrating our unique environment and heritage.

*w*e join in this tribute to our uniquely beautiful southwest. May we awake to its fragility and do all we can to preserve this ancient territory.

Pepsi Cola Bottling Company of El Paso

We are blessed with a wonderfully grand environmental park. Our mountains serve as a focal point for the reading of our wind and weather, a data point from which we locate ourselves in space and time. May our awareness of our environment be measured against these enduring peaks.

Our individual responsibility for our community can and should meet upon this "common ground."

Rick Kelly, ComputerLand of El Paso

*t*he Miles Group, the only full transport consortium in the area, provides a lot more than just transportation, warehouses, and employees to its corporate customers. Acting as a "good neighbor," Miles has made a stand in favor of both preserving the environment and conserving natural resources.

Miles handles all types of material, whether hazardous or not, according to the highest professional standards... because, as Mike Miles says, "We care about the environment." The company also acts responsibly in seeing to it that all laws are adhered to by its customers. Its transport fleet is kept properly maintained at all times to prevent air pollution, and all vehicles are retired after only 4 years service. To the Miles Group, being a good neighbor means more than contributing financial support to over 40 local charities and human services. It also means taking care of this earth we all share.

*k*PMG Peat Marwick is dedicated to preserving the proud heritage of our community through its commitment toward creating an environment which encourages individuals to achieve their full potential.

*P*erched atop a foothill of Mt. Franklin, overlooking the Rio Grande and downtown El Paso, Providence Memorial Hospital is more than just a modern health care center. For over thirty years Providence has co-existed in peace with its environment.

Beyond meeting federal standards for air cleanliness and waste disposal, Providence has gone the "extra mile" by establishing its own co-generation facility to recycle all energy needs. Over 2,000 Providence employees share a sense of common history with Mt. Franklin, a long-term association in which nature is not seen as an enemy of growth.

The Franklins and El Paso

Traveling through the desert southwest—the 'mountain-basin' country, as it's called—one finds a number of mountain chains much like the Franklins: seemingly barren, rocky, jagged peaks rising suddenly from flat desert floor. Who'd have thought this particular mountain chain would have a unique mission?

In the same travels one also finds a number of cities that at first resemble El Paso: Albuquerque, Tucson, Phoenix, Las Vegas—all share similar countryside and climate. All those cities are delightfully different in some ways, but most people, even El Pasoans, do not seem to realize that it's only El Paso that has a mission in life, and that mission gives El Paso a flavor like no other city.

Sometimes there's a bite in the flavor: El Paso whines that its museums can't compare with Fort Worth's or Tulsa's; that its Rio Grande has none of the tourist charm of San Antonio's RiverWalk; that its educational achievements can never match Austin's, etc. Why can't El Paso be Dallas-on-the-border? The reason is that El Paso has a different business, and different delights to savor.

El Paso's business is to blend two cultures that are very different; to patiently weave vast numbers of recent U.S. immigrants into the mainstream of the U.S. life while always affirming, and trying to incorporate, the wisdoms and beautiful ways of Mexico. The challenge (and the fascination) here—and it's being met very well so far—is to show the world how to build an enriched community out of, and because of, radically diverse elements.

But the Franklins' special job may be even harder to achieve. There they sit, surely as magnificent a wilderness as anywhere in the world, in aloof isolation at the heart of the teeming city. In a society gone mad with waste,

14

destruction, consumption and money, the Franklins' assignment is to stab into this society as they stab into the midst of El Paso, and teach us, each time we look up on them.

The influence of the Franklins on El Paso may be more subtle than, say, the influence of the Mississippi River on New Orleans, but in the same way, these giant natural phenomena teach us the important lesson that we are dwarfs in their power. If you want to feel the raw power of the Franklins, go and climb for a while on one of the slopes that look so easy.

On the other hand, these great things of nature make us finally realize that while we can never match their power we can easily destroy their beauty. Lakes get polluted—mountainsides get graded and defaced; and ever after that they serve as a reproach to us instead of an inspiration.

And, if we look, the desert mountains will show us a natural ecosystem as unusual and exquisite as any in the world. Every species of plant and animal is perfectly suited to its place and to each other so that a perfect natural harmony is offered. Quite an example those mountains set for us!

So El Paso and the Franklins, geographically intertwined by accident, now seem united in a destiny for great roles. Let's hope they both succeed, because the planet depends on it.

Bruce Hallmark

Our Franklin Mountains form the backbone of El Paso. They split the city down the middle, giving it a recognizable form. Without the Franklins, El Paso would be just another flatland place. But we do have the magic of our mountains, making our river-bend town unique.

Humans have walked the canyons of the Franklins, climbed their rugged slopes, since time's beginning. The Ones Who Came Before knew the secrets of these mountains, and the Indians, later-come, left their trails and signs throughout these folded hills. Along their flanks, heading north and then south, came the *puchteca*, ancient traders out of Mexico, carrying trade goods and parrot feathers to exchange for turquoise, the sacred stone. Came the Spaniards, marching north in search of Eldorado, leaving stark memories of bloodshed and hidden gold—always hidden gold—in their wake.

Our mountains have heard the bawl of cattle, legitimate and not. Cattlemen drove livestock north and south along the mountain flanks, and rustlers used Smugglers Gap, transformed now into Transmountain Road, as a short cut from the east side to the bosques of the Rio Grande. The bosques formed a tangled jungle of cottonwoods, mesquite and thorny scrub along the river banks, a sanctuary for those who knew the twisted, secret trails.

That's all gone now. The bosque disappeared with the taming of the river. But the mountains still stand sentinel above the scene, unchanged.

There's been gunshot echo through the Franklins. Ranger Charlie Fusselman was killed up there one day in 1890, and there's no telling

Alex Apostolides, Wilderness Park curator, listens to a message from Yesterday.

how many other men have left their bones in the mountains down the long, dry years.

The tales grow taller with each telling—silver and gold and old, dry bones. They're all up there, if you listen to the legends. And if even one-tenth of them are true, the Franklins hold a treasure trove as rich as any in the West.

The real treasures, though, the only ones worthwhile, are right in front of us every time we look.

Stand out there some early morningtime. Watch the first rays of the sun tip the crest, the shadows tumble down the canyons.

Watch and listen as the earth shifts gears and night time turns to day.

Hear the rising hum of bees as the sun warms all that tilted landscape—the clack of the roadrunner, the calling of the urgent quail.

A hawk comes swooping down to inspect you, there in early morning, and cactus wrens lift their voices from their nests in the blooming yucca.

Stand in the light and shadow of the Franklins, any time of day—and count yourself lucky to be here, part of this time and place.

Alex Apostolides

PHOTO: ALEX APOSTOLIDES

The mountains tip and tilt, remembering times when the earth moved. A "Clown face" kachina mask grins from a rockface at Hueco Tanks (right).

A Song of Time and Earth Unfolding

Old workings in Tin Mine Canyon.

PHOTO: ALEX APOSTOLIDES

Look at the tipped and tilted folds of the Franklins. What magic forces worked to bring these mountains into being? ¶ Once upon a time, 120 million years or so ago, a vast inland sea covered all this land, fed by the rains and the river we call the Rio Grande. That vanished sea is known to geologists as Lake Cabeza de Vaca, named for the first Spanish explorer to stumble this way, lost, in 1536. The waters of this one-time sea rose and fell for untold aeons, rich with teeming life. As generation after generation of sea life died, the shells and skeletons fell like dust motes in sunlight, building layer upon layer down the years, forming a sea bottom thousands of feet thick, changing into limestone as time rolled slowly by.

Meantime, other forces were groaning underneath the waters. As vents opened deep in the earth, magma came surging forth, sometimes in slow progression, infiltrating the limestone strata, sometimes in explosive force as molten rock met water and turned it into steam. Volcanos shouted in the air both north and west, and the face of the land was changed forevermore. One day the earth shrugged her shoulders, forcing gigantic blocks of landscape far above the surface. Old sea bottom and congealed volcanic flow tilted upward at the east, plunged down westward—and what we know today as the Franklin Mountains were born.

The Hueco Bolsón lay on one side now and, to the west, the bolsón of Mesilla. Deep sedimentary layers trapped and held the ancient waters—the waters our part of the Southwest drinks today.

You can read the story of the Franklins in the colors they display. The gray limestone is that ancient sea bottom, wracked and lifted up into the middle of the air, shot through with the fossils of marine life. The volcanic red-orange of rhyolite, memory of ancient molten rock thrust up from deep in the heart of the earth, intrudes upon the limestone gray. The formation

23

Gray limestone from ancient inland seas and deep volcanic red meet in the middle of the Franklins.

known as the Thunderbird, facing west across the river, is old rhyolite, exposed as the limestone strata weathered away. Great flat slabs lie tilted east to west, the upper end of that slanted limestone layercake forming the ridgeline of the Franklins. In the golden light of early evening, looking at the mountains from the west, you can see the effect of those great movements of the earth—the folding, twisting lines frozen now in space and time.

What we see now is only a remnant of that great uptilted land mass. The mountains have been weathering down through time, their sediment forming the fans and arroyos of the foothills, filling the bolsons east and west—carried away, grain by patient grain, on the waters of the Rio Grande. It's a rich and magic story, the way our Franklin Mountains came into being. ■

OVERLEAF: *Cottonwood Springs—an oasis in the middle of the mountains.*

Hikers cross a rockfall, memento of a landslide (opposite).

A 34 million year old rock. Spanish bayonet and beavertail (right). Limestone, manganese and garnet, part of our mineral treasures (below left).

Tin Mine Canyon is filled with shafts
and tunnels and ruined walls that
look like an ancient city.

31

The gateway to the morning side of the mountain—beginning of Transmountain Road, once known as Smugglers Gap. A scaled quail surveys his world from a cholla (right).

PHOTO: BARRY ZIMMER

PLANT AND ANIMAL LIFE

Another World, Just Waiting

There's light and shadow here, changing by the hour. You can spend a very busy day, just watching the play of light along the face of these near, dear mountains. Yet—as tires hiss along Transmountain Road, people in those cars never dream there's a timeless, other world living and breathing just beyond the pavement. A rich landscape lies just beyond the asphalt, waiting for you to get out and walk and see the treasures that it holds.

A hawk makes lazy circles in the sky, looking down on his domain. Far below, rabbits scurry through the chaparral and rattlesnakes begin to stir in the warmth of early-morning sun. There's the sudden call of quail as a covey breaks into startled, ground-skimming flight before disappearing into the underbrush. A flash of brilliant orange catches your eye—a dragonfly looking like a piece of captured sunlight flies past on whatever mission a dragonfly might have. Wasps hover in the air, drawn by the scent of water. They're yellow and orange and brown. Their big brother, the tarantula hawk, whirs by, body of shiny metallic blue-black, touched up by the brilliant red of lacy wings.

Peer underneath a leaf—there's a cocoon. Who knows what kind of winged wonder will emerge finally in the sun?

A pair of coyotes lopes easily down the draw. They pause to look you over and then go on their way—probably headed for the smug and settled blocks of the Northeast district, knowing of wonderfully fat small dogs there for the hunting.

That's the readily visible life. Get closer to the ground, and there's another world going busily about its day. Ants trudge back and forth in formation, bearing bits of leaf and other treasures to the underground

Poppies turn the foothill meadows into golden blankets after the springtime rains.

network they've laced into the mountain flanks. People often look at the Franklins and see only "desert." The early dwellers here looked on all the land as bountiful—their source of food, their pharmacy, their means of shelter.

Today, not that much has changed, although greasewood—the creosote bush—covers the lower slopes and terraces, sure sign of earth overgrazed and long disturbed. But let it rain, and the perfume of the greasewood fills the air, making it a sweet time to be riding along the lower slopes of the mountain.

Further upslope, the greasewood gives way to the darker green of mesquite. Mesquite beans made up an important part of the early dweller's diet—and two leaves, chewed, got rid of the most persistent headache.

Cacti in wondrous variety and form cover this land. Many of them are endangered species now, due to the insensate thrust of development along the flatter foothill reaches and the hunger of eastern markets for desert plants. More than 54 distinct varieties of cactus have been identified in the Franklins, and there are more just waiting to be found. If and when they are, the most probable discoverer will be Clark Champie, the biologist-author-artist who's tramped the Franklins for more than 30 years. His books, *Cacti and Succulents of the Franklins* and *Strangers in the Franklins* are standard guidebooks for the field.

Each cactus bloom is a miracle, no two of them alike. But the cacti provide more than a feast for the eye—they're source for food and drink, as well. The broad flat leaves of the *nopal*, the beavertail, make a succulent dish, cut into strips and cooked. And its fruit, the *tuna*, better known as prickly pear, has been rich foodstuff from time immemorial.

You'll find the *cholla* up here, the spines of which penetrate so swiftly that oldtimers swore it jumped out to get you. The Apaches used its yellow wrinkled fruit to make *tiswin*, a brew you could live all the rest of your life without tasting and not have missed anything.

Collared lizard, lichen and red-brown country rock.

The *lechugilla*, also known as the Spanish Bayonet, covers the limestone slopes. When you peel off your jeans after a hike in the Franklins, chances are you'll be surprised to see small red spots on your legs, souvenirs of spine-bite from the lechugilla. It's a small price to pay for the wonder of walking in our mountains. In spite of its bite, the lechugilla is a useful plant. Bend back the spine and peel it down the leaf, and you have an instant needle and thread.

The white flowers of the yucca are a rich food source, raw or cooked. The black seeds, taken from the round green pods, are rich in oil and minerals. The long and narrow leaves are prime stuff for basket-making, and the roots provide rich and soapy suds for washing or shampoo.

PHOTO: BARRY ZIMMER

There's the long green pine-needle look of the *ephedra*, known as squaw tea, Indian tea, Mormon tea, *canutillo*, *popotillo*—take your pick. Boiled green or dry, the tea's a mild stimulant and a stomach-settler. Pick a needle from the bush and chew it, and you'll find yourself hiking without getting tired far longer than you would without the mild boost of ephedra in your day.

The list is endless. Everything that lives or takes root in the desert has its place in the general scheme of things, plays its part in the teeming life of this seemingly barren landscape.

The arroyos shelter stands of cottonwood, leaves whispering in the wind. The vigas that span the ceiling of oldtime adobe homes were made from cottonwood—the seasoned wood will last forever.

Hawks—ferruginous (left) and red-tailed (right)—flank cotton fields and pecan groves on the west side of the Franklins.

Higher up the mountain, you can still find stands of ancient, twisted juniper, fossil remnants of a time when there was rain and a different world of green covered these slopes and rocky canyons.

It's a world all its own, the plant and wildlife of the Franklins, carrying on for the most part as it did for thousands of years before the first human poked an inquisitive nose over the horizon. May it carry on, this wonder-world, for several thousand years more. It could, you know, if only we leave it alone, appreciate it for the treasure house it is, sitting here in our own backyard. ▪

Biznaga candy's made from the barrel cactus (above). There are 35 different plants in this wild desert-mountain garden (opposite). See if you can find them.

39

The Swainson's hawk soars in the air of the Franklins. The land's alive with life that hovers, crawls and slithers.

41

*The seldom-seen porcupine lives in a
landscape filled with desert textures
and patterns unique to our Southwest.*

El Paso nestles against the mountain's flanks. We have a magic wilderness in our backyard. Sugarloaf in the middle distance; McKelligon Canyon slanting to the right. Cactus wears its winter-colors coat (right).

The Horned Lizard, misnamed the "Horny Toad," is a placid, friendly soul.

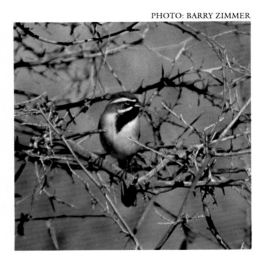

Each cactus blossom has a personality of its own. The century plant (opposite) bursts into bloom, a last explosion of color before it dies. Black-throated sparrow (above).

as the wind, following the game wherever it may lead. You're stuck to a plot of land—you are a "farmer" now.

Your horizon more restricted now, you begin to build shelters more permanent than a hut of twigs or a lean-to made of hides and branches. You dig a circular or D-shaped pit, entered by a ramp. Over it, you make an igloo-shaped form of twigs or branches and cover the whole thing with adobe mud. And, because you must live near your cornfield, the pithouses are built in clusters—and the first villages are born.

One year, there's a surplus, more corn than your small group can eat. Someone knows of another group, just over there beyond the mountains, whose women make pottery better than anything you have.

Let's take some of our corn over there and see…trade is born.

The hut-clusters grow and more people live past their childhood, now there's food enough for all. One day someone gets a bright idea—if we join the walls of our houses together, we'll save a lot of energy…and what we know as the pueblo comes into being.

Now a complicated society is in full swing—division of labor is well entrenched, and "civilization" is upon us.

One man makes better arrowheads than anyone else—fine; let him spend his time doing just that. You're better at hunting, and so you follow that skill. Someone else makes a better pot or basket…

…see how it grows? The simple, basic society of from each according to his ability, to each according to his needs is in full flower.

The people who lived here before us lived in a deep harmony with the rhythms of the Earth Mother. They were "animist," in the sense that everything had a spirit. The rocks, trees, the mountains…thunder, lightning and the soft and sudden miracle of rain—all these were holy things. They were recognized in song and dance and prayer, in symbols pecked and painted on the rock. We look upon these ancient art galleries and see messages from Yesterday—reaching across the years with the theme that Man is one with the planet upon which he lives, one life form among many, each with its own pride of place.

This ancient way of life, living in harmony with the earth and all her rhythms, lasted for several thousand years.

There were connections among those people the extent of which we are only dimly beginning to realize and appreciate today. Traders wore deep trails coming north from Mexico, bringing the religion of the Plumed Serpent, Quetzalcoatl, and of Tlaloc, the Goggle-Eyed God, with them. Bringing parrot feathers, copper bells and the magnificent ceramicware of the trading centers of Paquimé—Casas Grandes—and taking back turquoise and buffalo hides in return.

Men built their pithouse villages along the Rio Grande, below the Franklins along the foothills on the west and south. To the east, on ancient terraces, bedrock mortars were ground and pounded deep in the ironstained granite, and petroglyphs and pictographs were created in secret places among the rocks and in the canyons, along trails that had spiderwebbed the mountain for as long as men could remember.

All this was lost by the time the first Spaniards rode over the horizon, bringing with them the cross and the sword. The large groups of people here had dwindled and then disappeared some time around 1450, leaving only small remnants to greet the Spaniards when they came almost 200 years later, looking for mythical cities of gold.

Through it all, the Franklin Mountains remained unchanged. The hidden canyons with their ancient rock writing, the secret places are still there, witness to the passing of Man in space and time.

Mesquite beans—rich food source for the desert dweller...

…and the Rio Grande, bringing life to everything it touches.

One of the Old Ones, with the bedrock mortars of Whiterock Canyon.

56

The Sierra de Juárez stretches above our sister city on the other side of the Rio.

Wilderness Park Museum, where you take a walk through Yesterday (left).

*Day or night, the sky's alive in our
mountain-desert world.*

Mount Cristo Rey's a landmark along this winding stretch of the Rio Grande.

59

McKelligon Canyon has everything from back country trails to hidden caves to old rock houses to an amphitheater where the Viva, El Paso! pageant is presented every year. The face of the mountain changes with every passing season, every time of day.

North Franklin Peak (7192 feet) is the highest point in the Franklins and the second highest point in Texas.

Ephedra *(Mormon tea) in bloom. We see double rainbows in the Franklins every time it rains.*

Yucca juts from windswept dunes of sand while tadpoles swarm in here-today-and-gone-tomorrow rain pools. Iron stained granite and jungle-thick greenery along a magic trail, 15 minutes from the city just beyond (opposite).

Power lines make a spiderweb tracery of light up Hondo Pass…on the west side, the Potrillo Mountains form a backdrop in the fading light of day.

Red chile ristras *and cotton, twin treasures of the Southwest.*

Fields of grain and green chile harvest—bounty of the rich river bottomlands.

Nature's camouflage—Brother Coyote takes on the colors of the desert.

De Oñate took possession of this area in 1598; the Spanish influence is still with us.

74

4

The Search for Eldorado

They came north, the old Spanish explorers did—Espejo, Chamuscado, all the rest, looking for the Seven Cities of Cíbola, golden ghosts somewhere beyond the skyline.

They say Cabeza de Vaca stumbled past this way in 1536. If he did, the bulk of the Franklins certainly would have caught his eye, their southern end a finger pointing to the water of the Rio Grande. And, if he did, the people living here at the time—the Piros and Tampiros, the Mansos and their kin—must have shaken their heads in wonder at this White Eyes and his companions, lurching crazed and hairy and lost in a landscape the Indians have long called home.

Organized Spanish explorations began thrusting northward in 1581. The west side of the Franklins must have been witness to their passage. The Spaniards followed the course of the Rio Grande north, shunning the flatland that lies between the Franklins and Otero Mesa to the east. Little did they dream there was water across the bolsón at Hueco Tanks, a magic spot that had been a place of spiritual power for Man for thousands of years.

The thrust was north along the river, toward those fabled Seven Cities. Any settlement near the Franklins took place along the river, mostly beyond the southern tip of the range where it comes to a sudden end, broken by the valley of the Rio Grande.

The Spanish settlement lay along the north and eastern flanks of the Sierra de Juárez, just across the river. The first stones of the Guadalupe church were laid down there in 1598, and a market and way station established for the explorers headed north.

Though the mountains were not settled, they were hardly out of the picture. There are tales of Spanish treasure hidden in the Franklins. The Lost Padre Mine is probably the most famous. "If you stand in the tower

75

of the cathedral and look northward, where the black meets the red, there is where you will find the Lost Padre Mine...."

No chance of that today—and not for many years now...too many buildings have gone up to stand between the cathedral and the mountains.

And yet—we know of a man who spent seven years searching in the Franklins for the old Lost Padre Mine. He made meticulous sightings, drew maps of the "signs" he'd seen—markers leading one after the other, in his view, to the magic place where the Lost Padre still lies hidden.

And it may be true. We wish him luck, wherever he may be, because he's following his dream—and that's the only treasure worthwhile having.

If there *is* a Lost Padre Mine, it's most likely in the Organs, the rugged mountains lying to the north. And, most likely, it's somewhere in San Augustín Gap on the east side, where Father LaRue, the "lost padre," had his village and his fabulous mythic mine of gold.

But it's nice to look at the Franklins and speculate that *there*, just up there, where the red rock meets the black, *there* is where the Lost Padre must surely lie.

Our friend, the one who spent those seven years roaming far into the Franklins, thinks so—and who's to say he's wrong?

The Spaniards left far more than lost and hidden mines in the Franklins. Stories abound—

There's a cave somewhere up there, holding old and crusted rawhide bags filled with old gold coins. It exists—an old man, now in his 90s, found the cave when he was just a boy.

"Señor," he says. "I have never had to work a day in all my life. I found the cave when I was very small, tending sheep in the mountains. There were these dried-up leather bags in there, heavy with gold coins. I have been going up there all my life, every time I needed money. And I would take only what I needed. No one else ever found my cave, because it has been untouched, except by me, in all these years."

Somewhere in the Franklins there's a cave...

On the west side of the mountains is still another cache, this one of silver coins. It's the turn of the century. In a saloon in Canutillo, by the Rio Grande, where everyone is waiting for old Manuel, the shepherd, to come buy them drinks, paying for them with ancient silver coins.

When anyone would ask Manuel where he'd found the coins, he'd squint an eye and grin and, waving a finger in the air, order another round of drinks.

These mountains hold wagon-loads of lost and hidden treasure, to hear them tell the tales.

Some of the hangers on tried following him once or twice, but Manuel would disappear, not to be seen until his next trip into town, bearing more of the silver coins.

This went on for some time, Manuel showing up once a month or so, disappearing once the money had been spent, vanishing into the mountains where no man could find his trail.

One night the fiesta was going hot and heavy and Manuel wanted to keep on drinking with his friends. He left the saloon, promising to come back with more of those ancient silver coins.

Behind him, one bum caught another's eye, and they slipped out into the night, bent on finding the old shepherd's hiding place.

Manuel's battered body was found up an arroyo on the west side of the Franklins the next day. His killers, the two bums, had ambushed him and then, not being exactly genius calibre, had freely spent the silver coins in the saloon that night.

They were hanged, but not before being advised of the two big mistakes they'd made. The first was spending those silver coins so freely in a place where everyone knew their source. The second? They hadn't managed to catch up with Manuel until he was coming back from wherever he had gone.

Manuel's treasure trove of silver coins, somewhere on the west side of the Franklins, remains lost, a mystery to this day.

Larger battles were fought up and down in the shadow of the Franklins—again, most of them on the west side, the side along which the river flows. Doniphan's Missouri Volunteers whipped the Mexican army of Armijo here in 1846. The stories tell of the battle's having taken place 18 miles or so north of downtown, at the place called Vado.

78

But an eyewitness report seems to place the battle at a different location. James Kirker, a notorious bounty hunter, was coming back from a scalp-hunting raid in Mexico. Hearing the sounds of battle, he rode over a place where there were three low hills and saw the fighting going on beyond.

Now, there are three low hills at the southwest end of the Franklins, the only such formation anywhere around. A small bronze cannon was found in a dry limestone arroyo near those three low hills, and not too long ago, at that. And old brass buttons have been found in the immediate area, too, from the Mexican army uniforms of that time, so Doniphan's battle may well have happened there on that 1846 Christmas Day.

Vado…Franklins—take your pick.

Another bronze cannon—a small one, probably a mountain howitzer—was found at the north end of the Franklins, where they dip to form Anthony Gap. Two hikers, just noodling around, stumbled upon their prize. They hid it up a box canyon, raced down to town to come back with a jeep.

You know what happened. They never could find that box canyon again. And so, somewhere in a box canyon on the north side of the Franklins, a small bronze cannon sits, waiting for someone else to come along and find it.

Still another cannon, this one huge, was found—and lost again—somewhere on the east slope of the Franklins, near the spot where a large "A" stands out in painted white against the slope. That, and a cache of gold coins, seen once and sample taken—and then never found again.

Yep, there are treasures lying up there in the hidden reaches of the Franklins, all right.

All you have to do to find them is go out and look...

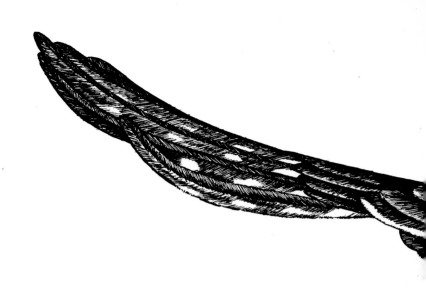

A golden eagle flies high above the Franklins, higher than the bird-men flying down below.

PHOTO: BARRY ZIMMER

80

*Steep trails and views all the way to
the far horizon reward hikers in the
Franklins. Ephedra (Mormon tea)
grows thickly in our mountains (right).*

OVERLEAF: *The Thunderbird is an El Paso landmark, a volcanic intrusion in the ancient limestone of the mountain.*

Yellowbell, a splash of color in
Whiterock Canyon.

OVERLEAF: *William Beaumont*
Army Medical Center stands out
against the Chinese-painting backdrop
of the Franklins.

PHOTO: ALEX APOSTOLIDES

Fire sweeps our mountains now and again—but new growth is never far behind.

PHOTO: BARRY ZIMMER

A jackrabbit cocks an attentive ear. Everyone loves a roadrunner (left). A desert tortoise comes to look us over (below left).

5

1 8 8 0 TO TODAY

Sixguns, Wagon Trains, Iron Rails and Pavement

hings changed for good in 1880. That's the year the railroads came, and the face of El Paso, sitting wrapped around the south end of the Franklins, was never the same again.

The village had been named Franklin, after Benjamin Franklin Coons, a trader who'd set up shop and a hotel to take advantage of the trade flowing west toward California's Gold Rush. The town's name went through many changes before "El Paso" was finally settled on, but "Franklin" has remained the name given to the mountain range that splits the city.

The old Santa Fe-Chihuahua Trail flanked the Franklins along their west side. To the east, dirt roads snaked their way northward, headed for the mining town of White Oaks and the Sierra Blanca villages of Lincoln and San Patricio, scene of the Lincoln County War of 1878, whose most notorious participant was William Bonney, "Billy the Kid."

Most of these years, the Franklins were the haunt of cattle rustlers and men on the run from whatever law existed. Smugglers Gap, paved now and called Transmountain Road, saw a steady clandestine traffic from the east side to the river as herds of stolen livestock were driven through to the safety of the tangled bosque that lined the Rio Grande.

Men went into the mountains, seeking fortune. Most of them came back out again with nothing more to show for their labor than callused hands and a raging case of sunburn. The mountains do not give up their secrets easily.

In 1903, scratching on the west side began, as fools with more hope than sense went burrowing into the mountain's flanks in search of whatever they could find. They found tin ore—but it assayed out at three cents a ton, and that made it hardly worth the trouble. A jackrabbit hole above Tom

Mays Park on the west side remains as memento of that illusion of easy, sudden wealth.

On the east side, hope sprang anew in 1910, when Tin Mine Canyon was the brief home of the only producing tin mine in the United States—and it was a controversial one at that.

The tin was there—it was actually produced, first in 1910 and again during World War II, but rumors clouded the efforts of 1910, with tales to the effect that the bulk of the tin was smuggled in from Bolivian mines and displayed as a home product to fleece gullible investors.

A man named Woodyard first found tin in 1896, but nothing happened for three more years, until a mining man named Morton showed up on the scene and the Florilla Mining Company was born.

A local banker sunk his hooks into the operation. He sent for experts to examine the locale and find out what it was he had.

The first ore samples the U.S. Geological Survey tested at the end of 1900 were a pleasant surprise—the ore was loaded with tin oxide. The government sent another geologist west to take a closer look, with the banker acting as host and Native Guide.

The geologist saw a beautiful vein of native ore—but it pinched off about fifteen feet down, cut by an earth slip or fault. Fair enough—the mother lode had to be somewhere far below. W.H. Weed, the geologist, was reminded of the great tin mines of Wales, where surface veins stemmed from huge mother lodes deep below the surface, 3000 feet and more.

We don't hear much about the Great Franklin Mountain Tin Discovery for the next four years or so. A rich prospect is well and good—but developing it takes money, and this is what the banker's group now set about.

Banker's scam or legitimate operation—the question has hovered around the tin-mining operation ever since. Whatever the case, the investors came flocking, and in 1909 the newly named El Paso Tin Mining and Smelting Company was born.

It had a brief and stormy history. During its two short years of existence, the mine shipped out some eight tons of smelted tin. The tin brought in a little less than $7000 for an investment of half a million dollars—and even the most stupid of investors could see he was in a losing game.

The mine closed down in 1911 and was the plaything of the banks and courts for the next six years. December 4, 1917 saw everything finally being sold at auction from the county courthouse steps, the bank's $21,000 bid giving them the property.

A sanitarium for infants briefly flourished on the site in 1921, but it soon failed for lack of support.

And then...nothing.

A mining survey was run in the 1930s, but that was it for the next 12-odd years.

Tin Mine Canyon saw a brief flurry of activity in 1942, with a world war on and the country's normal sources all cut off. A 100-foot shaft was sunk and seven tons of ore sent to the smelter in Texas City—but then another expert came along and said it was all a waste of time. Those veins of ore were shooting off in all directions, pinching out and showing up again; the price of getting it out of the ground was just too high.

The tin mine in the Franklins was shut down once again and lay abandoned after that, the buildings slowly crumbling down the years.

In 1958, the bank offered the property to the city of El Paso, to be used

Nesting baby hummingbird.

as a city park. It was a lease with an option to buy. Tin Mine Canyon could have been a city park today, commemorating the only tin deposit ever to be developed to the point of mining, milling and smelting at one location in the United States.

But you know what happened—the city fathers sat on their hands and more years passed, the buildings tumbling down a little more with every passing season.

Yet today, a quiet sign at the mouth of Tin Mine Canyon stands as token of a near-miracle. Franklin Mountains Wilderness State Park, it says. Someone, somewhere, cared enough to act—the old tin mine is now part of a state park that stretches from Transmountain Road northward to the place where the landscape dips to form the Anthony Gap.

It wasn't easy. A handful of people got together because they saw what was happening to the mountains under the impact of runaway "development." They banded together as the Franklin Mountains Wilderness Coalition and began a fight that has lasted to this day.

They looked at the fate of natural wonders in other places, determined they would not let it happen here. They phoned. They wrote letters. They carried the fight to the state capital in Austin—and they won in 1987; the Franklin Mountains Wilderness State Park is a reality today.

In the meantime, other good people saw the treasure the mountains hold for El Paso, the daily dangers that the mountains face, and they swung into action. Fort Bliss, whose Castner Range sprawls up the east slopes of the mountain, traded seventeen acres to the city in 1976 for the building of Wilderness Park Museum. Fred Hervey, onetime mayor of El Paso, donated $150,000 of his own money for the construction of the museum that stands there today.

New homes nestle in the shadow of the mountain.

Although it's been called "the best kept secret in El Paso," Wilderness Park draws some 30,000 visitors a year. They come to walk through a series of dioramas showing the adaptation of Man to a desert environment. The museum carries one from the time of the Early Hunters, when mammoth and other huge game trampled through a landscape much wetter than it is today, to scenes of a time when the rains slackened and then did not fall at all, and Man found himself a desert dweller.

The traveler through time sees a scene from Hueco Tanks, the power spot, the magic place where water's always found, and where pictographs and petroglyphs tell of Man's passage down the years. Another diorama shows a pithouse, looking much as it might have in its heyday 600 years ago, and a whole stretch shows "Olla Cave," a pueblo cliff dwelling high in the Sierra Madre of Chihuahua.

The area around the Franklins was heavily under the influence of Paquimé—Casas Grandes—a city and trading center of some 20,000 people whose trade routes wrapped around the Franklins, extending far to the north and west and east. Cave Valley, the narrow stretch of river canyon where Olla Cave is found, was a daughter settlement of the great city of Paquimé, and so its ties to the Franklins are well established.

An indoor/outdoor museum, Wilderness Park features a mile-long Nature Trail that winds along the foothill slopes, with replicas of a pueblo ruin, a kiva and a pithouse spread along the way. One day it may be part of the larger state park—for now, it continues as a museum run by the city.

Plans for the future of the Franklins are big and bold—and coming closer to reality every day. Reachable within 15 minutes from any part of town, our mountain range is an oasis. The trails twist and wind through the shadowed canyons and run along bare ridge tops. They take you into

99

*Thunderheads pile high above a
passing squall.*

a time before Yesterday when the only noises were the sound of rising wind, the boom of thunder echoing in the sky…into a place of dappled light and shadow, bare rock and the iron-hard spines of lechugilla giving way to the miracle of Whispering Springs, a place of mystery with the gleam of water and green growth in the middle of the dryness.

And somewhere up there—if the tales are true—lie hidden treasure, silver and gold and old dry bones, mementos of the men who passed this way before.

The Franklins—a treasure house sitting in the middle of our landscape, dominating the skyline and the lives of the people lucky enough to be living within touch. A treasure house we must cherish and protect for all time to come, a legacy to hand down to our children and everyone who comes thereafter. ■

Whispering Springs—a small jungle at the top of a high, dry canyon where deer come every morning.

102

The Apache made tiswin, *an alcoholic drink, from the fruit of the cholla cactus.*

The snows of winter blanket the Franklins—and then are gone almost as swiftly as they came.

The obelisk in El Paso's Tom Lea Park marks the beginning of the Rockies.

The sky is a constantly changing palette, at any time of day.

*Living on the edge—El Paso below,
Juárez out beyond—in a landscape
that never stays the same.*

Hueco Tanks

Look eastward from the Franklins. That hump breaking the long, low, limestone line of Otero Mesa is Cerro Alto. This side of it, to the west, is where you'll find Hueco Tanks. ¶ The Hueco Bolsón, lying between the mountains and the mesa, was covered by an inland sea several million years ago. The sea ran dry. The pocket left behind, the *bolsón*, was slowly filled with soil runoff from the Franklins to a depth of more than 1600 feet. It, like the Mesilla Bolsón west of the Franklins, is one of the aquifers, the reservoirs of fossil water, from which El Paso and much of Juárez get their drinking water.

Hueco (pronounced WAY-co) means a hollow or hole in Spanish. Hueco Tanks is the remnant of a volcanic plug of syenite porphyry exposed through the millennia as the ancient sea bottom slowly eroded away. The rock is pitted with hollows where water gathers after rain, making the place an oasis in the middle of the dry land all around.

Humans have been drawn to the Hueco Tanks for at least 10,000 years, as far as we know, and probably for long before. The water here provides the magnet.

Because water is an especially sacred thing in the desert, the place became a place of spiritual power, an area favored by the gods of the mountains and the desert, where ceremonies were held to celebrate the miracle of rain.

Traces of that old time religion are found everywhere you look at Hueco Tanks. You'll find pecked petroglyphs and painted pictographs all through the rocks and caves of Hueco Tanks. They range from the archaic times of the hunters and gatherers to the relatively sophisticated painted designs and masks of the Pueblo people known as the Jornada Branch of the Mogollón. Later in time, the Apache came and left their marks, as did

PHOTO: ALEX APOSTOLIDES

The volcanic upthrust holds caves and hidden passageways. Some of the huecos hold water all year long.

the Kiowa, ranging in from the plains country farther east.

More than 5000 petroglyphs and pictographs have been found at Hueco Tanks so far, with no one knows how many more waiting to be found.

The people who came to live at Hueco Tanks somewhere between 900 and 1400 AD were the busiest artists of all. Kachina masks were their most frequent subject, along with mythical beasts and other beings.

The designs were painted on the mother rock with pigments found within arm-reach. The reds and yellows are various oxides of iron; the blacks came from manganese dioxide, or from the black lichen which grows in every watercourse and forms along the cliff face wherever water comes dripping down. The white pigments come from caliche, calcium carbonate, also left behind as water evaporates.

Green pigment has been found on only one design at Hueco Tanks, the "clown face" at site 10 (see photograph on page 22).

The people who lived at Hueco Tanks in that golden age between 900 and 1400 AD were water control specialists to equal any engineer today. They enlarged existing drainage patterns, rubbing grooves in the bedrock to channel the water into reservoirs or down to their cornfields below.

Early Man was here long before. The people we know only as the Folsom, from their magnificent fluted projectile points, prized today by collectors, ranged far and wide through this ancient landscape, hunting the big game, the mammoth and the bison, that lived here in the time of much more rain.

As rainfall declined the big game disappeared, and the Folsom hunters along with it.

Came a people now who dug D-shaped or circular pits in the ground and roofed them over with domes of branches and twigs. Those early pithouses developed into adobe huts, built partly above the ground and, finally, into the connected rooms that formed the pueblos we know today.

They developed their own style of pottery. Their decorative pottery is known as El Paso Polychrome or El Paso Black on Red. Examples are rare, but they may be seen today at the Wilderness Park and Americana Museums in El Paso.

They developed their own system of water control. It seems highly likely, though, that the system of water engineering was inspired from Paquimé, the sophisticated center of trade to the southwest.

The mountains of Chihuahua are filled with rock baffles cleverly arranged to stop any flash flood before it starts, directing the flow of water to the fields below.

PHOTO: ALEX APOSTOLIDES

We know that the puchteca, traveling traders, branched out from the great centers of civilization in Mexico. They traveled up from Paquimé along the Rio Grande, entered the farthest reaches of what is now Utah and Colorado and ranged far east and west, bringing copper bells and parrot feathers and the distinctive painted pottery of Casas Grandes, taking turquoise and buffalo hides back home with them.

The early farmers, the settlers at Hueco Tanks, disappeared one day. Where they went or what made them go, no one really knows. Maybe there was a year in which the rains did not come, a year in which the prayers were ineffective. We find traces of their villages, their pueblos, all through the desert, silent witness to the people who lived here long ago. The Spaniards who passed this way in the late 1500's found only nomadic groups living around Hueco Tanks.

Later on, the Mescalero and Lipan Apache used the tanks as home base, raiding settlements along the Rio Grande and farther south. They, too, made their marks here. The Comanche and Kiowa came also, and the latter-day Tiguas came to the tanks to camp and hunt and hold religious ceremonies.

The early Spanish expeditions tended to stick to the river route along the Rio Grande, avoiding hostile Indians out at Hueco.

Hueco Tanks saw fairly quiet times after that, until about 1848. That's when the war with Mexico came to an end and the Treaty of Guadalupe Hidalgo was signed, establishing the Rio Grande as the international boundary.

What happened then was, literally, the opening of the West.

Texas towns had long been eyeing the lucrative Santa Fe-Chihuahua trade, and the discovery of gold in far-off California made them eager to find a southern, snow-free route across the country to the west. Three expeditions were sent out in 1848 and 1849 to find a route to El Paso from either Austin or San Antonio.

The first one, led by Texas Ranger Samuel Highsmith and John Coffee Hays, got lost in the Big Bend country and had to turn back.

Austin merchants sent out a second expedition, led by Dr. John Ford, nicknamed "Rip," and Col. Robert Neighbors, a Texas Indian agent.

The expedition outlined a road that roughly paralleled the present Texas-New Mexico line after crossing the Pecos River. The road went from Alamo Spring in the Cornudas Mountains through Hueco Tanks and El Paso, and it became known as the Upper Road.

The third expedition opened up the lower, or Military Road, by way of Forts Stockton, Davis and Quitman.

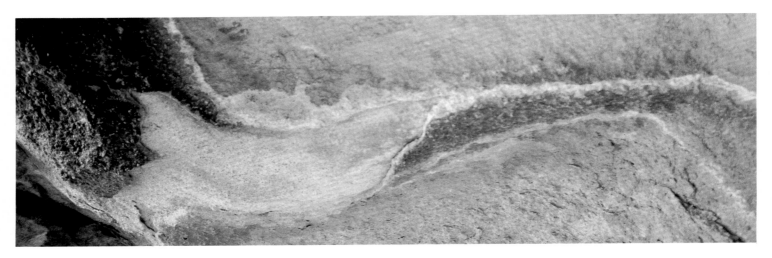

Ancient water-control channel.

One who traveled here was Benjamin Duval Harris, who wrote *The Gila Trail: the Texas Argonauts and the California Gold Rush.* Harris was a member of the party led by Capt. Isaac H. Duval.

The Duval party was one of the first to cross Texas on its way to California. It consisted of 52 men mounted on horses and leading pack mules. The Duval group met Col. Neighbors' expedition at Horsehead Crossing on the Pecos River, and then continued west by way of Hueco Tanks.

The first serious effort to record the Hueco rock writing was by U.S. Boundary Commissioner, John Russell Bartlett. He wrote a fascinating two-volume report with an extremely long-winded title (see Further Reading).

The Butterfield Overland Mail established a stage station at Hueco Tanks in 1858. From Hueco, the route ran down to what is now Overland Street in El Paso. The town wasn't called El Paso then; it bore the name of Franklin. The real El Paso was just across the river—El Paso del Norte, later re-named Juárez.

All the traffic was shifted later to the Lower Road, which was better protected by military posts. That was the time of the Apache, when you could literally lose your scalp traveling through unprotected country. But there were still travelers along the upper way, because names from the 1860's and 1880's are found at Hueco, pecked or scratched into the rock.

In modern times, the plague of the desert, the land developers, descended on the scene. A huge earthen dam was bulldozed into being between the West and North Mountains of the tanks, completely destroying what may have been a prehistoric Indian village there. The whole place was going to be Disney-fied, with a Frontier Town and a lake, a golf course and

a zoo. Happily, the wild visions of the developers were shot down in mid-flight, as El Paso County got the property in the mid-60's, operating it as a county park, complete with concessionaires. Later, the Texas State Legislature made it a State Park.

Hueco Tanks State Historical Park, which now covers some 860 acres, was opened officially to the public in May 1970. It operates today under the watchful eye of the Texas Parks and Wildlife Rangers, who look on it as a treasure held in trust for the thousands of people who come to visit—and for their grandchildren yet to come. ■

Looking westward from Hueco Tanks, the Franklins punctuate the far horizon.

The Franklin Mountains State Park

The following groups and individuals are specifically mentioned for their contribution and character in the establishment of the park: Franklin Mountains Wilderness Coalition ∎ Concerned Citizens of Northeast El Paso ∎ District IV of the League of United Latin American Citizens ∎ El Paso Archeological Society ∎ El Paso Cactus and Rock Club ∎ El Paso Color Camera Club ∎ El Paso Regional Group of the Sierra Club ∎ El Paso/Trans-Pecos Audubon Society ∎ El Paso Wilderness Preservation Committee ∎ El Paso Women's Political Caucus ∎ Friends of the Franklins ∎ League of Women Voters of El Paso ∎ Mesilla Valley Audubon Society ∎ Mountain Park Association ∎ Northeast El Paso Civic Association ∎ Southwestern New Mexico Group of the Sierra Club ∎ Tularosa Basin Group of the Sierra Club ∎ Westside El Paso Civic Association ∎ Gerald Fitzgerald ∎ Mike Bilbo ∎ Jeff Donaldson ∎ Le Bron Hardie (Sierra Club Special Achievement Award) ∎ John Sproul (Sierra Club Special Service Award) ∎ John Colburn ∎ Carol Hedrick ∎ Joan Duncan ∎ Wesley Leonard ∎ John Green ∎ Malcolm Harris ∎ Ronald Coleman, U.S. Representative ∎ Tati Santiesteban, past Texas Senator ∎ Jack Vowell, Texas Representative ∎ City Representatives in early 1989: Jim Goldman, Suzie Azar, Tony Ponce, Jethro Hills and Ed Elsey.

The Franklin Mountains State Park is an urban wilderness park located in the heart of El Paso, Texas. The park was created by the Texas Legislature in 1979. Boundary amendments enacted in 1981, 1987 and 1989 place the park's current acreage at 23,925, probably making it America's largest urban park. Funding for staffing and operation of the park was granted in 1985.

More recently, the Bureau of Land Management (BLM), U.S. Department of Interior, was convinced to preserve the Franklin Mountains in New Mexico as a natural area, commonly referred to as the BLM Preservation Area, containing 13,191 acres. In addition, the BLM has preserved a corridor of land between the Franklins and the Organ Mountains, the Organ/Franklin Corridor, for wildlife migration and ecological systems to continue to interact and maintain wilderness capability. The corridor contains 5360 acres. Combining the federal and state land area for the Franklin Mountains, a total of 42,476 acres are now protected.

However, the exact interpretation of the term "protected" has not been determined yet. Usage of the park must be defined by a master plan. The agency responsible for the plan's development is the Texas Parks and Wildlife Department. Within this agency, a professional unit will give serious consideration to all aspects of the master plan, such as whether the park should be delegated to pure Wilderness status, whether equestrian trails should be provided, or recreation vehicles allowed, or hotels constructed for tourists, or even whether mule trains operated by the park officials should be allowed. Those issues are by no means all-inclusive. The master plan will be thoroughly detailed in allowances and restrictions; therefore, interested individuals and groups should contact the Texas Parks and Wildlife Department if they wish to participate in and/or influence the framework of this plan. ∎

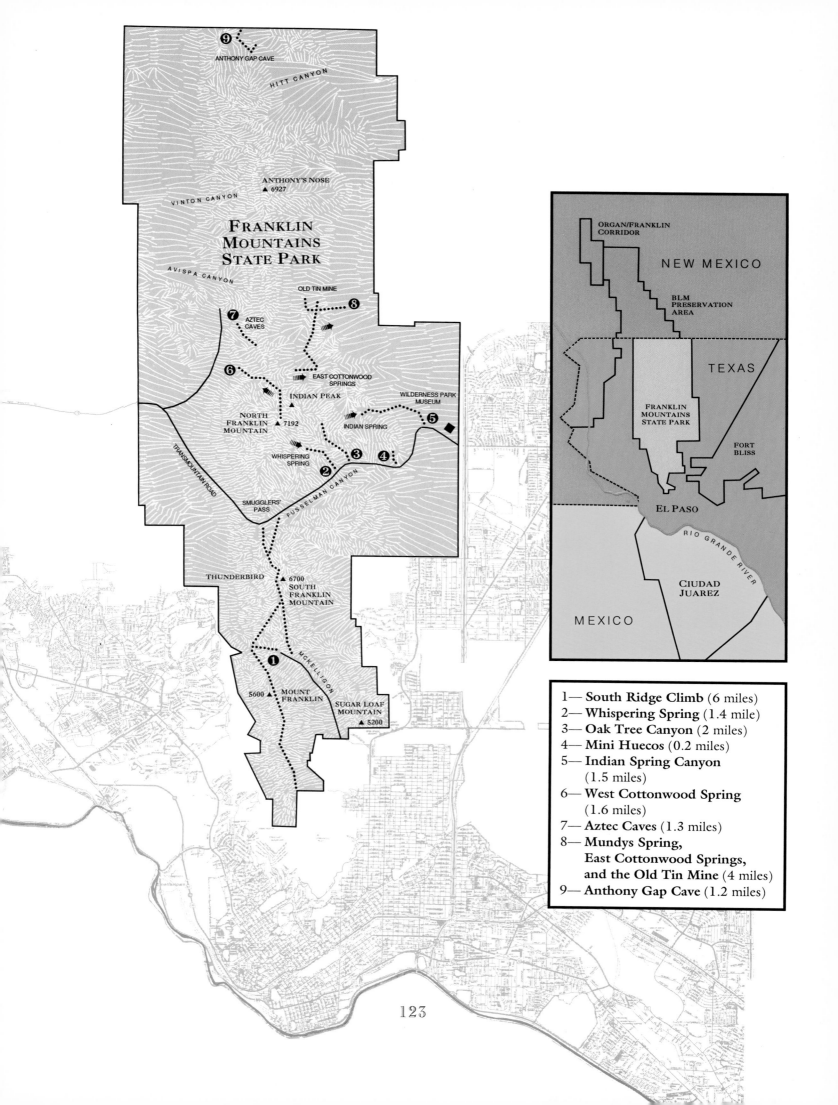

❾
ANTHONY GAP CAVE

HITT CANYON

ANTHONY'S NOSE
▲ 6927

VINTON CANYON

FRANKLIN
MOUNTAINS
STATE PARK

AVISPA CANYON

OLD TIN MINE

❼ AZTEC
CAVES

❽

EAST COTTONWOOD
SPRINGS

❻

INDIAN PEAK
▲

WILDERNESS PARK
MUSEUM

NORTH
FRANKLIN
MOUNTAIN ▲ 7192

INDIAN SPRING

❺ ◆

WHISPERING
SPRING

❸ **❹**

❷

TRANSMOUNTAIN ROAD

SMUGGLERS'
PASS

FUSSELMAN CANYON

THUNDERBIRD
▲ 6700
SOUTH
FRANKLIN
MOUNTAIN

❶

McKELLIGON

5600 ▲ MOUNT
FRANKLIN

SUGAR LOAF
MOUNTAIN
▲ 5200

❾
ANTHONY GAP CAVE

ORGAN/FRANKLIN
CORRIDOR

NEW MEXICO

BLM
PRESERVATION
AREA

TEXAS

FRANKLIN
MOUNTAINS
STATE PARK

FORT
BLISS

EL PASO

RIO GRANDE RIVER

CIUDAD
JUAREZ

MEXICO

1— **South Ridge Climb** (6 miles)
2— **Whispering Spring** (1.4 mile)
3— **Oak Tree Canyon** (2 miles)
4— **Mini Huecos** (0.2 miles)
5— **Indian Spring Canyon**
    (1.5 miles)
6— **West Cottonwood Spring**
    (1.6 miles)
7— **Aztec Caves** (1.3 miles)
8— **Mundys Spring,**
    East Cottonwood Springs,
    and the Old Tin Mine (4 miles)
9— **Anthony Gap Cave** (1.2 miles)

GLOSSARY

Anasazi — "The Ones Who Came Before." This was the name given by the Pueblo people to the ancient inhabitants of the Southwest.

bolsón — (bol-SOHN) From the Spanish, *bolsa*, or "pocket." The Hueco and Mesilla Bolsons are the "pockets" left by an ancient inland sea and the upheaval of the Franklin Mountains some 34 million years ago.

bosque — (BOSS-kay) Spanish for *forest*. The bosque was the tangled growth of everything from pussy willow to mesquite that lined the banks of the Rio Grande before the river was tamed inside concrete channels. The bosque was a favorite hideout for bandits and cattle rustlers.

Lincoln County War — The players in New Mexico's Lincoln County War—Billy the Kid, John Tunstall, Alexander McSween, the Murphy-Dolan gang, all passed into the realm of folk legend. The "war" began on Febuary 19, 1878 with the ambush murder of John Tunstall. It ended with Billy's murder by Pat Garrett at Fort Sumner on July 14, 1881.

mano — (MAH-no) Spanish for *hand*. The hand-held stone used to grind corn into flour on the *metate*.

metate — (meh-TAH-teh) The stone slab on which corn is ground, using the *mano*.

petroglyph   Prehistoric design made on rock faces by pecking, cutting or rubbing.

pictograph   Prehistoric design made on rock faces by painting, using mineral or vegetal pigments.

Puchteca   (Poosh-TECK-ah) Aztec traders who filtered through all of Mexico and up into what is today's Southwest. They brought trade goods (ceramics, parrot feathers, copper bells) with them, along with their religion of the Plumed Serpent.

tiswin   (TISS-win) Alcoholic drink made by fermenting the fruit of the cholla cactus. An Apache drink. The Tarahumara Indians of the Barranca del Cobre in Chihuahua made tesguino (tess-GWEEN-oh), an equally evil-tasting beverage, from corn.

viga   (VEE-gah) Roof beams. Logs are laid on the top of the adobe walls, spanning the area to be roofed. Branches and twigs are laid on top of the vigas and then the roof is completed by piling dirt on top.

Further Reading

Bartlett, John R. *Personal Narratives of Explorations and Incidents in Texas, New Mexico, California, Sonora and Chihuahua.* 2 volumes. New York: US-Mexican Boundary Commission. 1854.

Bryson, Conrey. *The El Paso Tin Mine.* The Password. Vol. 3 No. 1. El Paso, Texas: El Paso County Historical Society. 1958.

Champie, Clark. *Strangers in the Franklins.* El Paso, Texas: Guynes Printing Co. 1973.

Hirsch, Dena. *Union of Eagles: El Paso/Juárez.* El Paso, Texas: Rainbow in a Tree Publications. 1987.

Jackson, A.T. *Picture Writing of Texas Indians.* Publication No. 3809. Austin, Texas: University of Texas Press. 1938.

Lovejoy, Earl. *El Paso's Geologic Past.* Science Series No. 7. El Paso, Texas: Texas Western Press. 1980.

Newcomb, W.W. Jr. *The Rock Art of Texas Indians.* Austin, Texas: University of Texas Press. 1967.

Sonnichsen, C.L. *Pass of the North.* 2 volumes. El Paso, Texas: Texas Western Press. 1968.

————— *The Mescalero Apaches.* Norman, Oklahoma: University of Oklahoma Press. 1958.

Timmons, W.H. *El Paso: A Borderlands History.* El Paso, Texas: Texas Western Press. 1990.

A true precolumbian artifact in the Franklins...six thousand feet above sea level, this second millenium juniper tree still stands today. It was already 500 years old when Columbus sailed to America.